FAIRY TALE PRINCESSES & Storybook Darlings
Coloring Book

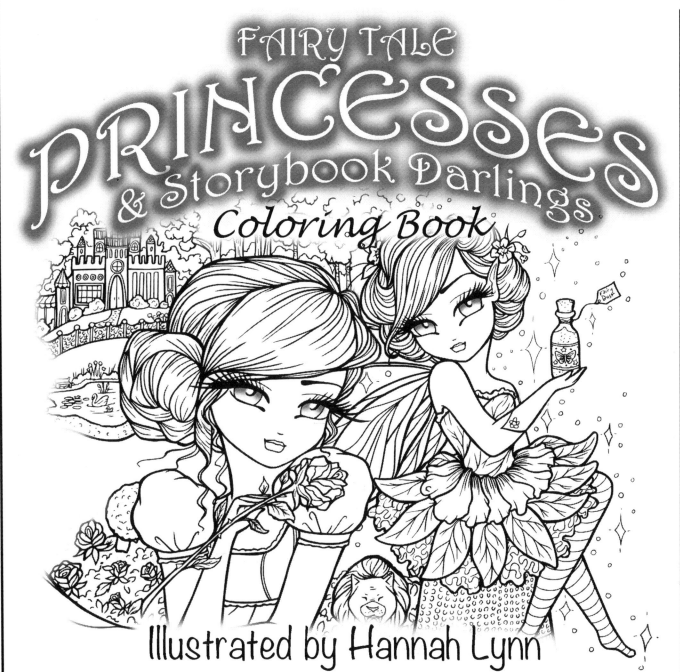

Illustrated by Hannah Lynn

www.HannahLynn.com

© Hannah Lynn Art & Design 2018

All Rights Reserved. Personal Use Only. No Redistribution.

Coloring Tips
from Hannah Lynn

Place a small stack of copy paper (4-5 sheets) behind the page you are coloring on to eliminate bleed-through and indentation marks to other pages in your book.

You don't have to commit to using just one medium like markers or colored pencils. You can use all kinds of materials on just one coloring page. Gel pens, glitter pens, markers, colored pencils, and crayons can all work great together! Really wet mediums like paints are not recommended for this type of paper, but I do offer a PDF printable version for sale on HannahLynn.com for those that prefer to use their own paper!

If you prefer to work with markers, consider using colored pencils for larger background or flesh tone areas in a light, circular motion for more even coverage (markers can sometimes leave unwanted streaks over large areas). You can always add more layers of colored pencil to achieve your desired depth of color.

There are no rules with art! The grass doesn't have to be green, tree trunks don't have to be brown, and the sky doesn't have to be blue. Have fun with it, and if you feel that you have made a "mistake", don't fret! Every artist, including myself, experiences a period of uncertainty during each piece. Art is fluid. If you keep going, you will see that it works out in the end and gain more confidence from seeing it through! If you feel like you need a break, come back to it with fresh eyes later. Since there are two copies of each illustration in this book, you can experiment in different ways!

The best way to improve your skills is through experience. So get your materials out, turn on some music that inspires you, and HAVE FUN!!!

For more tips and tutorials, please visit my website at HannahLynn.com

Follow me @hannahlynnart on Facebook, Instagram, & Twitter! Please visit my Author Page on Amazon.com (Hannah Lynn) to view all of my available coloring books, journals, and more!

www.HannahLynn.com

© Hannah Lynn Art & Design 2018

All Rights Reserved. Personal Use Only. No Redistribution.

"Off to the Ball" "To Grandmother's House" "To be Human" "Princess & the Pea" "Hansel & Gretel"

"Little Miss Muffet" "Magic Carpet Ride" "Snow White & Friends" "Down the Rabbit Hole" "Fairy Godmother"

"Mermaid Lagoon" "Pinocchio's Wish" "Rapunzel's Tower" "Off to See the Wizard" "The Frog Prince"

"Afternoon Croquet" "Enchanted Rose" "Straw into Gold" "Waiting for Peter Pan" "Morning Chores"

"Tinkerbell" "Goldilocks" "Briar Rose" "Thumbelina" "The Big Day"

Made in the USA
Columbia, SC
26 February 2025

54446139R00059